CONTENTS

Whatever you choose to make first, you'll need plenty of packaging. So it's a good idea to start collecting it in advance. Ask people to save things for you instead of throwing them away.

You can flatten cardboard boxes and cereal boxes to save space. Rinse plastic bottles and leave them to dry. Prepare an area to work in, and have lots of old newspapers handy if you are using glue and paints.

HOW TO MAKE MAGIC AMULETS

Amulets were sacred lucky charms for the living and the dead. The ankh was the hieroglyphic symbol of life. It meant health and happiness. The eye of Horus, or wedjat eye, was a powerful protection against evil. The scarab beetle was the most popular amulet. It was the symbol of birth and eternal life.

YOU'LL NEED:
Scissors, tracing paper, masking tape, pencil, paper, PVA glue, cardboard, paints, felt-tips or metallic pens, and decorative string or magnetic strip.

1. Copy the templates onto paper (see the instructions on the inside front cover).

2. Glue them onto a piece of cardboard, cut around, and decorate with the paints and pens.

3. Paint over with a mix of half water and half PVA to give a shiny finish. Allow to dry.

4. To hang your amulet, glue the ends of the string onto the back. Cover them by gluing another piece of cardboard over the top.

5. To make a magnet, cut a piece of magnetic strip to size and stick on the back.

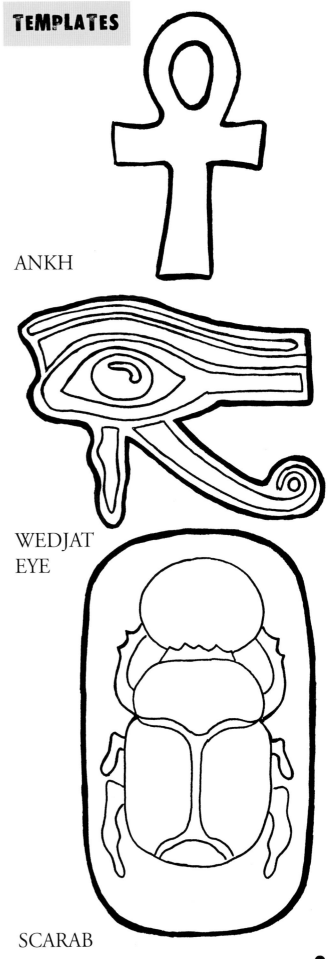

ANKH

WEDJAT EYE

SCARAB

WHO PUT THE "Y" IN PYRAMIDS?

Egypt is known for its pyramids. The most famous are the pyramids of Giza, and the biggest of them is the Great Pyramid. It is the first, and last remaining, of the seven wonders of the ancient world.

We think it was built as the tomb to beat all tombs for the Pharaoh Khufu (or Cheops).

I was there, but I'm not telling.

SPHINX

It is 479 feet (146 m) high and was the biggest building in the world for nearly 4,500 years.

It's still the heaviest at 6.6 million tons (6 million t)!

It contains about 2.3 million blocks of stone. Each weighs about 2.2 tons (2 t).

The outer stones fit so perfectly that a knife can't be pushed between them.

Inside are secret passages leading to a central burial chamber.

PYRAMAGIC

In the Middle Ages, it was thought that the stones had been flown into position after being put on sheets of papyrus like magic carpets.

Left a bit.

PYRAMAD?
Today, people with unusual ideas about the pyramids are called pyramidiots.

They think that spacemen built them…

…or the man from Atlantis, (a lost land drowned by the Great Flood)…

…and that the ancient Egyptians sailed over to America in a papyrus boat and showed the Mexicans how to build their pyramids.

Muchos graciás.

PYRAMEX

The very first pyramid was built about 2650 BC to be the tomb of Pharaoh Zoser.

It was seen as his stairway to heaven when he died.

How did the ancient Egyptians make something so big yet have such accurate measurements?

They had only copper, stone, and wooden tools.

Ow!

We think they floated giant stones down the Nile on barges and then along canals to the pyramid.

Then the stone blocks were levered onto wooden sleighs, wooden rollers, or round stones.

Finally they were pulled up ramps built around the pyramid.

Watch the corner!

Ramps made of small stones or mud bricks.

But nobody has fully explained how the Great Pyramid was built. See what you can find out.

Using the wonders of today, like robots, satellites, and DNA, we are learning more and more about the wonders of the past. Soon, someone will solve the mysteries of the Great Pyramid. It could be you!

PYRAMEDICS

HOW TO MAKE A PYRAMID

Try to make your own Great Pyramid. Make a small one first to see how it works, and then make a bigger one. It could even be big enough to get inside and frighten people using a ghostly voice! Give your Great Pyramid an aged look by tearing off the paper in places to show the corrugations underneath. Use your paints to make it look old or new.

YOU'LL NEED:

Scissors, craft knife, glue, ruler, pencil, tracing paper, masking tape, ballpoint pen, thin cardboard, large piece of corrugated cardboard, and thumbtack.

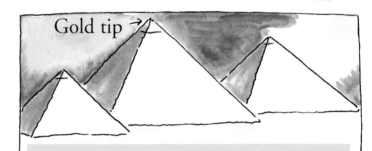

Gold tip →

WHEN THEY WERE NEW, THE PYRAMIDS WERE COVERED IN BRILLIANT WHITE LIMESTONE, WHICH WOULD HAVE GLINTED IN THE SUNLIGHT. WHAT A MAGNIFICENT SIGHT!

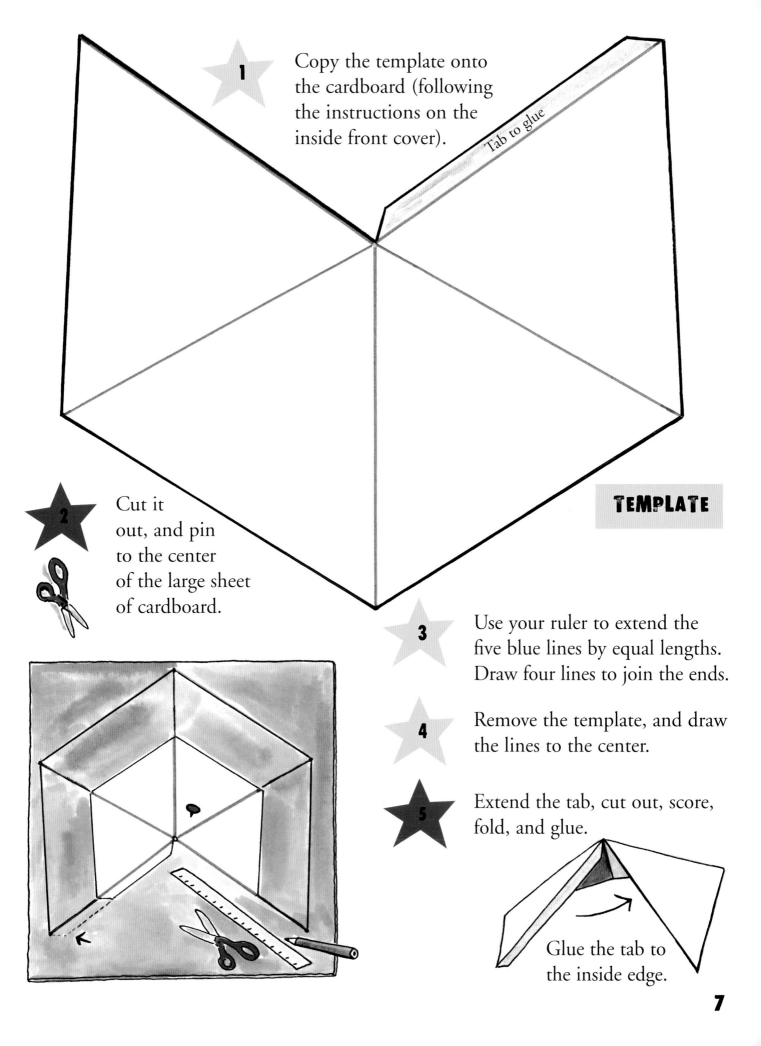

Tab to glue

1 Copy the template onto the cardboard (following the instructions on the inside front cover).

2 Cut it out, and pin to the center of the large sheet of cardboard.

TEMPLATE

3 Use your ruler to extend the five blue lines by equal lengths. Draw four lines to join the ends.

4 Remove the template, and draw the lines to the center.

5 Extend the tab, cut out, score, fold, and glue.

Glue the tab to the inside edge.

7

HOW TO MAKE A POP-UP MUMMY

The ancient Egyptians believed in life after death, but only if their bodies were perfectly preserved. These were embalmed and wrapped in linen bandages. The preserved body was called a mummy.

YOU'LL NEED:

2 sheets thin cardboard, pencil, tracing paper, masking tape, ballpoint pen, scissors, ruler, double-sided tape, paints, and felt-tips.

EVERYONE LOVES MUMMIES. THEY ARE FUNNY AND SCARY. THE FIRST MUMMY FILM WAS MADE OVER 100 YEARS AGO!

Tut toot!

Happy Mummy's Day!

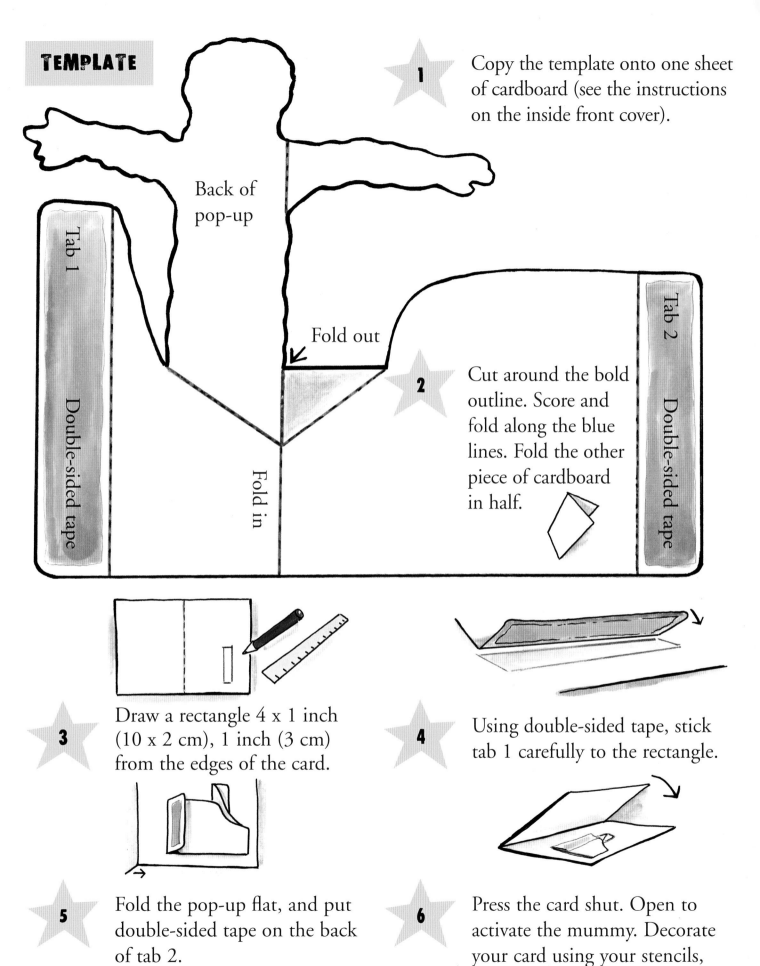

TEMPLATE

Back of pop-up

Tab 1

Double-sided tape

Fold in

Fold out

Tab 2

Double-sided tape

1 Copy the template onto one sheet of cardboard (see the instructions on the inside front cover).

2 Cut around the bold outline. Score and fold along the blue lines. Fold the other piece of cardboard in half.

3 Draw a rectangle 4 x 1 inch (10 x 2 cm), 1 inch (3 cm) from the edges of the card.

4 Using double-sided tape, stick tab 1 carefully to the rectangle.

5 Fold the pop-up flat, and put double-sided tape on the back of tab 2.

6 Press the card shut. Open to activate the mummy. Decorate your card using your stencils, paints, and felt-tips.

DRAW LIKE AN EGYPTIAN

There is nothing quite like Egyptian art. The artists had to follow strict rules. They drew using a square grid, and each part of the body would take up its correct number of squares. If someone in the picture was important, that person was drawn larger than the others!

YOU'LL NEED:

Graph paper, ruler, pencil, paints, and gold and silver pens.

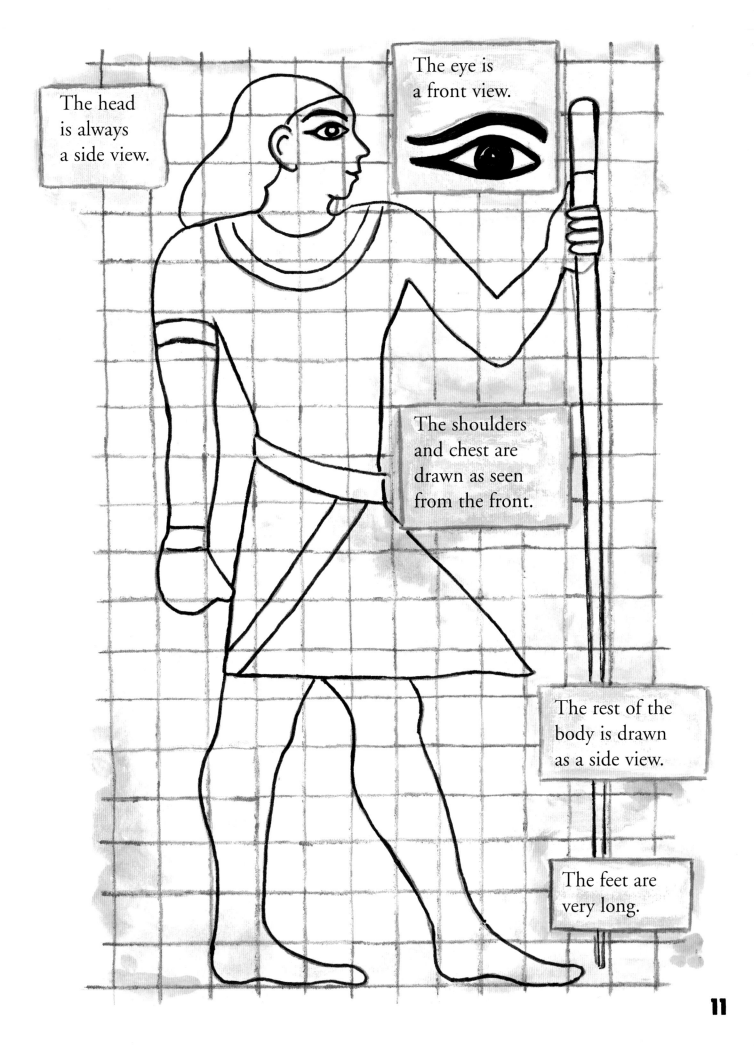

The head
is always
a side view.

The eye is
a front view.

The shoulders
and chest are
drawn as seen
from the front.

The rest of the
body is drawn
as a side view.

The feet are
very long.

11

ANCIENT EGYPT

Egypt is the world's largest oasis. A thin strip of fertile land, it stretches for 745 miles (1,200 km) along the banks of Africa's longest river, the Nile. The ancient Egyptians called their country "the gift of the Nile." The fertile black land by the river they called Kemi. The harsh, endless desert that hemmed them in they called Desret, the red land.

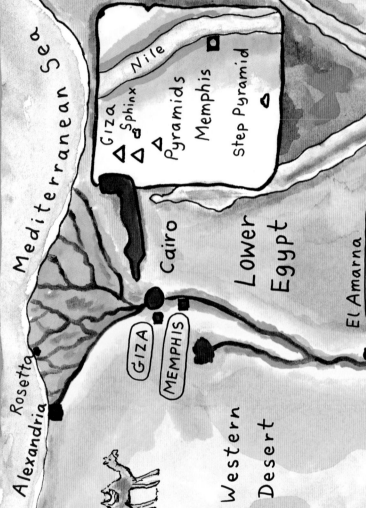

Mediterranean Sea

Alexandria

Rosetta

Cairo

GIZA

MEMPHIS

Giza
Sphinx
Pyramids
Nile
Memphis
Step Pyramid

Lower
Egypt

El Amarna
AKHETATEN

Western
Desert

BC.

3100 BC
Earliest recorded history of Egypt. Hieroglyphs first used.

Walking fish glyph. (No translation yet!)

2700–2400 BC
The Great Pyramids built at Giza (near Cairo).

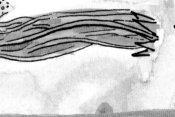

AD

AD 1799
The Rosetta Stone is found, which leads to Champollion cracking the code to reading the hieroglyphs in AD 1832.

Champion, Champollion!

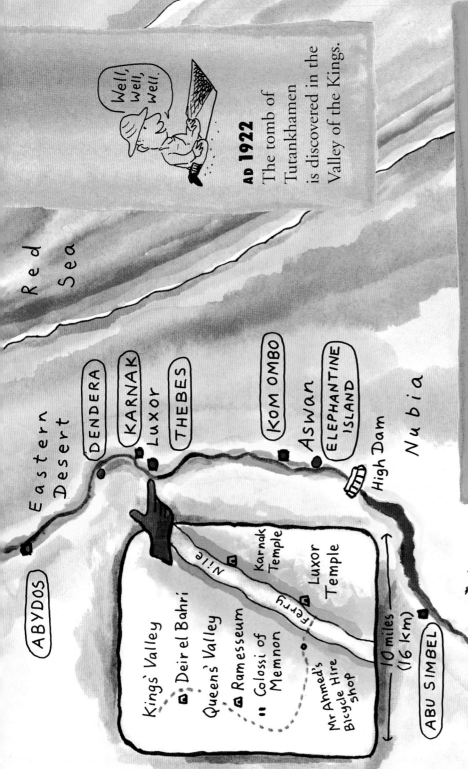

AD 1922
The tomb of Tutankhamen is discovered in the Valley of the Kings.

Well, well, well.

Rain is almost unknown in this strange land. The fields are watered by ditches bringing water from the Nile. Before the building of the great dams at Aswan, the Nile flooded every year. This left the fields covered with rich, dark, fertilizing mud that came all the way from the heart of Africa.

Red Sea

Eastern Desert

DENDERA

KARNAK

Luxor

THEBES

KOM OMBO

Aswan

ELEPHANTINE ISLAND

High Dam

Nubia

Sudan

ABYDOS

Nile

Karnak Temple

Luxor Temple

Ferry

Kings' Valley

Deir el Bahri

Queen's Valley

Ramesseum

Colossi of Memnon

Mr Ahmed's Bicycle Hire Shop

10 miles (16 km)

ABU SIMBEL

1350 BC
The boy-king Tutankhamen buried in Kings' Valley or Valley of the Kings (near Luxor).

30 BC
Cleopatra, last queen of Egypt, dies. Egypt becomes part of the Roman Empire.

Ouch!

HOW TO MAKE ANCIENT EGYPTIAN SWEETS

The Egyptians did not have sweets as we know them. Although sugarcane is grown along the Nile today, there was no sugar in ancient Egypt. So people used honey, dates, or fruit juice to sweeten food. This ancient recipe was found written on a piece of broken pottery.

THE ANCIENT EGYPTIANS USED GROUND CUMIN. IT MAY NOT BE TO YOUR TASTE, SO WHY NOT PUT HALF THE MIXTURE IN ANOTHER BOWL AND ADD 1/8-1/4 TEASPOON TO ONE AND MIX IN WELL.

KITCHENWARE YOU'LL NEED:
Food processor, large bowl, large plate, 2 teaspoons, tablespoon, and small muffin liners.

INGREDIENTS YOU'LL NEED:
7 ounces (200 g) stoned dates, 4 ounces (125 g) walnut pieces, 4 tablespoons clear honey, 1 teaspoon ground cinnamon, ground cumin (optional), and ground almonds for coating.

14

1 First, wash your hands.

2 Ask an adult to help with using the food processor. With the machine set to high, chop the dates until they form a ball (about 15 seconds). Take them out and put into the bowl.

3 Put the walnuts in the machine and chop for about 10 seconds. Put the dates back into the processor with the walnuts.

4 With the machine set to medium, add the honey and cinnamon through the funnel.

5 Put the mixture back into the large bowl.

6 Pour some ground almonds onto the plate. Roll a teaspoonful of mixture in them until well coated. Use two teaspoons to do this.

7 Put the sweets into small muffin liners.

HOW TO MAKE A JEWELED COLLAR

These beautiful collars were worn by both men and women. Kings, queens, and very rich people wore collars made with gold and precious stones. Poorer people made them out of flowers. When the flowers died, they made another one!

YOU'LL NEED:

15 x 15 inches (40 x 40 cm) white fabric, PVA glue mixed with water 1:4, paintbrush, old cardboard, masking tape, pencil, felt-tips, clothespins, scissors, and string or cord.

1 Lay the material over the old cardboard and paint with PVA mix. Leave two corners so you can pick it up. Hang up to dry. This may take several hours.

2 When dry and stiff, line up with the book, secure with masking tape, and trace the template in pencil.

3 Move the material around, line up, and trace again. Repeat until you've done it four times.

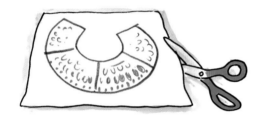

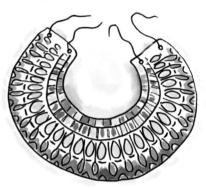

4 Color with felt-tips. Go around each shape with black to give a bold effect. Then cut out.

5 Make four holes and thread with string or cord for a fastening.

TEMPLATE

Line up corner of material with corner of the page.

HOW TO MAKE DECORATIVE ARMBANDS

As well as collars, the ancient Egyptians liked to wear armbands and bracelets, decorated in patterns of bright colors.

YOU'LL NEED:
Plastic drink bottle about 2–3 inches (5–7 cm) wide, scissors, craft knife, rough sandpaper, acrylic paints including white, and metallic pens.

1 Wash the bottle and remove the label.

2 Get an adult to help you cut a strip from the bottle.

3 Cut through, and round off the corners.

4 Rub sandpaper all over the plastic. Paint with white acrylic paint.

5 When dry, use acrylic paints and pens to decorate with an Egyptian pattern.

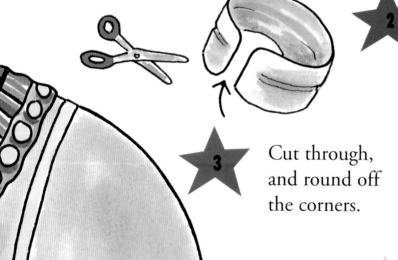

HAVE FUN WITH HIEROGLYPHS

The ancient Egyptians invented one of the very first written languages—a picture language of beautifully drawn birds and animals—called hieroglyphs. The stencil sheet at the back of this book contains 27 glyphs known as the hieroglyphic alphabet. Each one stood for a sound. Pages 20–21 show how they look painted on the walls of tombs and temples. Underneath there is a guide with approximate sounds in English. You can have fun writing English in hieroglyphs, just like a secret code.

HIEROGLYPHICS CAN BE WRITTEN VERTICALLY OR HORIZONTALLY. IT'S UP TO YOU!

THEY ALSO WROTE ON PAPER MADE FROM A REED CALLED PAPYRUS.

TIP BOX

There are over 700 different glyphs. See if you can find out the meanings of some more.

Don't worry, nobody knows exactly how ancient Egyptian sounded.

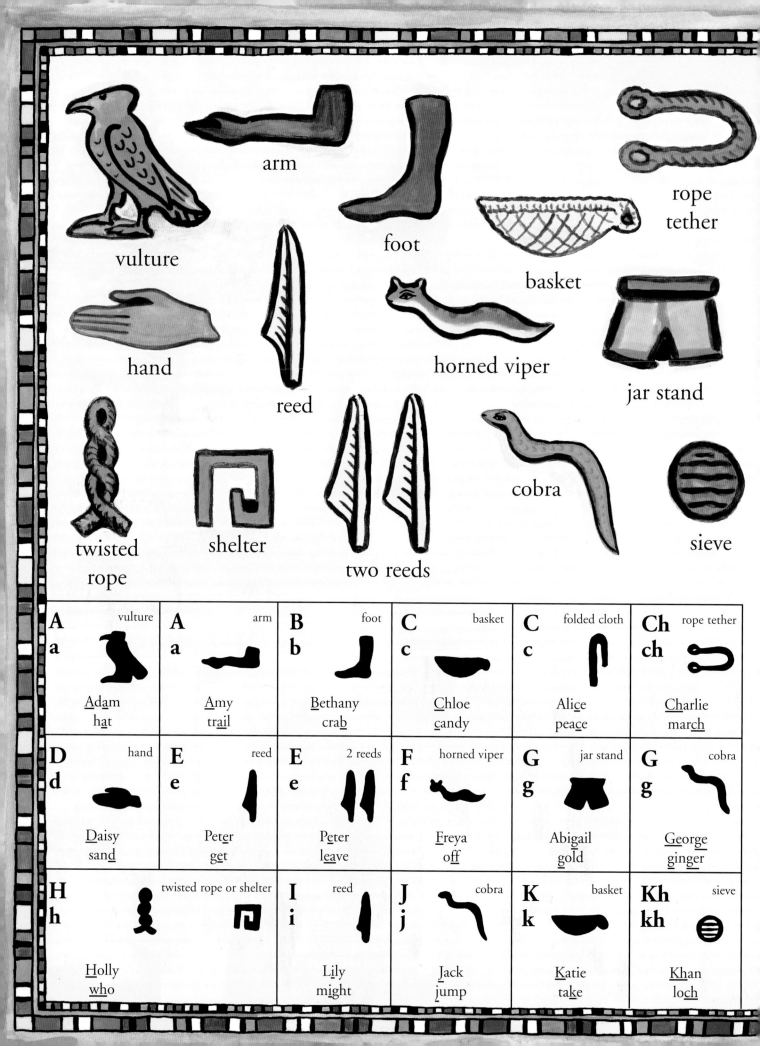

vulture

arm

foot

rope tether

basket

hand

reed

horned viper

jar stand

twisted rope

shelter

two reeds

cobra

sieve

A a	A a	B b	C c	C c	Ch ch
vulture	arm	foot	basket	folded cloth	rope tether
Adam ha**t**	Amy tr**ai**l	Bethany cra**b**	**Ch**loe candy	Ali**c**e pea**c**e	**Ch**arlie mar**ch**

D d	E e	E e	F f	G g	G g
hand	reed	2 reeds	horned viper	jar stand	cobra
Daisy san**d**	Peter g**e**t	Peter l**ea**ve	Freya o**ff**	Abigail **g**old	**G**eor**g**e **g**inger

H h		I i	J j	K k	Kh kh
twisted rope or shelter		reed	cobra	basket	sieve
Holly w**h**o		L**i**ly m**i**ght	**J**ack **j**ump	**K**atie ta**k**e	**Kh**an lo**ch**

lion

owl

water

lasso

door

slope

mouth

folded
cloth

lake

loaf

animal belly

quail chick

door bolt

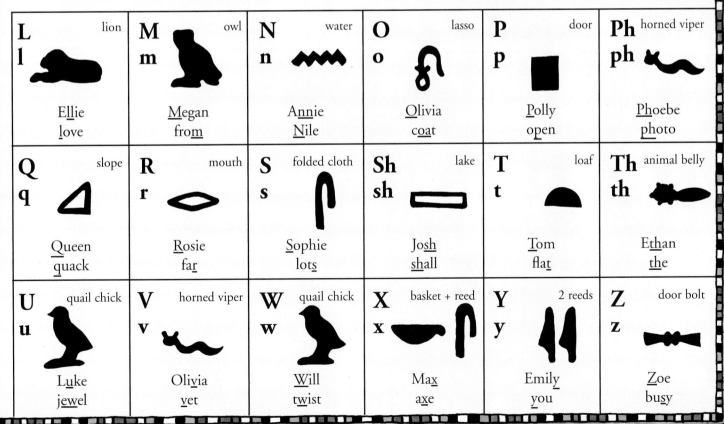

L l — lion	**M** m — owl	**N** n — water	**O** o — lasso	**P** p — door	**Ph** ph — horned viper
Ellie love	Megan from	Annie Nile	Olivia coat	Polly open	Phoebe photo
Q q — slope	**R** r — mouth	**S** s — folded cloth	**Sh** sh — lake	**T** t — loaf	**Th** th — animal belly
Queen quack	Rosie far	Sophie lots	Josh shall	Tom flat	Ethan the
U u — quail chick	**V** v — horned viper	**W** w — quail chick	**X** x — basket + reed	**Y** y — 2 reeds	**Z** z — door bolt
Luke jewel	Olivia vet	Will twist	Max axe	Emily you	Zoe busy

HOW TO MAKE A CARTOUCHE

The names of pharaohs were written inside a rope loop called a cartouche. Let everyone know whose room it is by making a cartouche for your bedroom door. You may have to translate it underneath—not everyone can read ancient Egyptian!

YOU'LL NEED:
Paper, pencil, ruler, jar, scissors, cardboard, paint and felt-tips, glue, and double-sided tape.

DISCOVERING THE NAME OF CLEOPAT(D)RA IN A CARTOUCHE HELPED TO SOLVE THE MYSTERY OF THE HIEROGLYPHS. THEIR MEANING HAD BEEN LOST FOR 1,500 YEARS.

Q CLEOPATRA D

IT WAS LIKE SOMEONE RECORDING THEIR LIFE ON VIDEOTAPE, THEN BUYING A DVD PLAYER AND FORGETTING HOW TO USE THE OLD MACHINE.

1 Choose the hieroglyphs from pages 20–21 that match the sounds in your name.

2 Draw them lightly in pencil on the paper.

3 Use the ruler to draw a frame around the hieroglyphs.

4 Use the bottom of the jar to draw the corners.

5 Paint or use felt-tips to color the hieroglyphs. Use pages 20–21 as a guide.

6 Paint or use felt-tips to make the frame look like rope.

7 Glue the cartouche onto cardboard, and cut it out.

8 Stick to your door using double-sided tape.

HOW TO USE YOUR STENCILS

Cut or tear off the stencil sheet from the back of the book. Choose a shape and place it over your paper. Hold it in place with masking tape. Draw the outline with soft pencil. The ancient Egyptians carved hieroglyphs into stone, so this will give your shape a shadow effect. Use pages 20–21 as a guide to coloring your shapes.

1 Hieroglyphs can be read in four different ways but are always read from the way the birds and animals are facing. You can turn your stencil over to make the shapes face the other way.

cobra > 2 reeds > water > chick

2 Experiment with colored paper, different textures of paper, and wax and colored crayons.